The Role of Neuro-Linguistic programming in Enhancing Resilience and Coping Skills

By Rex Morton

Disclaimer

This book is intended to provide information about the fields of Neuro-Linguistic Programming (NLP) and Cognitive Behavioural Therapy (CBT) and their potential integration. While the author has made every effort to ensure that the information was correct at the time of publication, the author does not assume and hereby disclaims any liability to any party for any loss, damage, or disruption caused by errors or omissions, whether such errors or omissions result from negligence, accident, or any other cause.

The contents of this book should not be used as a substitute for professional advice, diagnosis, or treatment. The reader should always consult with a qualified healthcare provider about any mental health concerns or conditions. Never disregard professional psychological or medical advice or delay in seeking it because of something you have read in this book.

The views expressed in this work are solely those of the author and do not necessarily reflect the views of the publisher, and the publisher hereby disclaims any responsibility for them.

The inclusion of websites, links, or references to other resources does not mean that the author or the publisher endorses the information the organization or website may provide or recommendations it might make. Furthermore, the author does not guarantee the accuracy of the information these resources provide.

The use of any information provided in this book is solely at your own risk.

1.1 The Birth and Evolution of Neuro-Linguistic Programming

The inception of Neuro-Linguistic Programming (NLP) traces back to the early 1970s. It was a brainchild of Richard Bandler, a psychology student, and John Grinder, a linguistics professor, both hailing from the University of California, Santa Cruz. Their shared curiosity led them to model the strategies of several effective communicators and therapists of that time, like Fritz Perls, Virginia Satir, and Milton Erickson. They observed and replicated the behavioral patterns of these successful individuals, which culminated in the establishment of NLP as a unique field.

In its initial stage, NLP focused on therapeutic applications. However, as it evolved, it expanded its reach to various other areas, including personal development, education, business, and sports. The core principle remained the same: using language and mental imagery to influence an individual's thoughts, feelings, and behaviors. Over the years, NLP has undergone several revisions and transformations, adjusting to the shifts in understanding about human cognition and behavior, yet retaining its initial essence.

1.2 The Imperative of Resilience and Coping Skills

In the dynamically challenging world we inhabit today, the ability to adapt to stress and adversity, known as resilience, and the capacity to manage stressful situations or hardship, referred to as coping skills, are invaluable. The speed and complexity of life's demands can, at times, be overwhelming. It is during these instances that resilience and coping skills become our allies, providing us with the mental agility to navigate through life's challenges and come out stronger on the other side.

The capacity to 'bounce back' from misfortune and keep one's mental health is resilience. It does not imply avoiding stress or living a life devoid of adversity. Rather, it's about learning to cope with these challenges effectively and perhaps even learning and growing from the experiences. Coping skills, on the other hand, are the strategies or techniques that individuals use to manage stress and adversity.

1.3 The Intersection of NLP, Resilience, and Coping

So, how does Neuro-Linguistic Programming fit into the equation of resilience and coping skills? The essence of NLP lies in the understanding and transformation of our subjective experiences. It provides tools and techniques that enable us to better understand our thoughts, emotions, and behaviors. By offering ways to reframe our experiences, NLP empowers us to transform our perception of challenges and stressful situations.

With its focus on self-awareness, positive reframing, and goal setting, NLP aligns seamlessly with the foundations of resilience and coping. By mastering NLP techniques, one can effectively enhance their resilience by shaping their belief systems, developing mental agility, and cultivating a positive mindset. Additionally, the use of NLP strategies can augment our coping skills, helping us navigate through adversity with greater ease and less distress.

As we delve further into this book, we will explore these intersections in greater depth, uncovering the myriad ways in which the principles and techniques of NLP can be harnessed to fortify our resilience and enrich our repertoire of coping skills.

Chapter 2: Understanding Neuro-Linguistic Programming

2.1 What is NLP?

NLP, or neuro-linguistic programming, is a communication, personal growth, and psychotherapy technique that looks at the connection between language, cognition, and behavior. It offers doable suggestions for how to alter our thinking patterns, perspective on the past, and outlook on life.

The term 'Neuro-Linguistic Programming' is a reflection of the interconnectedness of our mental, linguistic, and behavioral patterns:

'Neuro' refers to our nervous system, through which our experiences are processed via our five senses.
'Linguistic' signifies the use of language and how it influences our experiences and those of others.
'Programming' denotes the behavioral patterns we learn and develop over time.

2.2 Core Principles of NLP

While the approaches and techniques within NLP are numerous, they are all guided by a core set of principles:

The Map is Not the Territory: This principle acknowledges that our perception of reality is not reality itself but our 'map' or mental model of it. Our experiences, beliefs, and values shape this map, and each person's map is unique.

Experience has a Structure: Our thoughts, feelings, and behaviors follow patterns, and by changing these patterns, we can change our experiences. This principle is at the heart of most NLP techniques.

If One Person Can Do Something, Anyone Can Learn to Do It: This principle highlights the idea that we can model the successful behaviors and mindsets of others to achieve similar results.

The Mind and Body are a Linked System: There is a connection between our thoughts, feelings, bodily sensations, and behaviors. When one thing changes, other things may follow.

The Meaning of Communication is the Response You Get: This principle emphasizes the importance of flexibility in our interactions. If we're not getting the response we want, we should change our approach.

There is No Failure, Only Feedback: This encourages a growth mindset, viewing 'failures' as learning opportunities.

2.3 The Structure of Subjective Experience: The Triad of Neurology, Language, and Programming

The key to understanding NLP is to grasp how it views the structure of our subjective experience. It is based on the triad of neurology, language, and programming:

Neurology represents our biological and physiological processes. It's how we engage with the world through our senses and how these sensory experiences influence our thoughts and emotions.

Language is our primary system of symbols and meanings. It's the tool we use to order our thoughts and communicate our experiences. NLP explores how the words we use can affect our mental states and behaviors.

Programming is the set of learned behaviors and coping strategies we've adopted over time. NLP provides techniques to 'reprogram' these patterns to achieve more desirable outcomes.

The interplay of these three components forms our subjective experience. By understanding and manipulating this triad, NLP offers tools to change our perception and response to life's challenges, which is the basis for enhancing our resilience and coping skills. As we continue our exploration in the following chapters, we'll discover how this fascinating process works in practice.

3.1 What is Resilience?

Resilience, in the psychological context, refers to the ability of an individual to recover from adversities or difficult situations and bounce back to their original state, or even a better state of mental well-being. It involves endurance, flexibility, and strength in the face of stressors, traumas, or significant sources of threat.

Resilience does not mean one does not experience hardship or distress, rather, it is about the ability to adapt and respond effectively to these difficulties. It's an ongoing process that requires effort and time. It comprises protective factors—such as a positive self-concept, problem-solving skills, and a supportive environment—that equip individuals to withstand, confront, and learn from life's adversities.

3.2 What are Coping Skills?

Coping skills, or coping mechanisms, are strategies that individuals employ to deal with stressful situations, adversities, or negative emotions. These strategies aim to mitigate, manage, and adapt to stressors, helping to restore emotional balance and minimize the harmful impact of stress on mental and physical health.

The two primary categories of coping techniques are problem-focused coping and emotion-focused coping. Problem-focused coping is aimed at addressing the root cause of the stressor, seeking to change or eliminate it. On the other hand, emotion-focused coping targets the emotional distress associated with the situation, seeking to alleviate the emotional impact of the stressor.

3.3 The Interplay between Resilience and Coping

Resilience and coping skills are intertwined, often working in harmony to support individuals through adversities. Resilience acts as a buffer against the adverse effects of stress, while coping skills provide the practical strategies used to manage and navigate through challenging situations.

Coping skills are an essential aspect of resilience. The more effective an individual's coping strategies, the more resilient they are likely to be. These strategies facilitate adaptation to adversity, thus enhancing resilience. Conversely, resilience can improve the effectiveness of coping strategies. Individuals with high resilience are often more equipped to implement and benefit from positive coping strategies.

Understanding the relationship between resilience and coping is crucial when exploring how Neuro-Linguistic Programming (NLP) can be used to enhance these aspects of our mental well-being. The principles and techniques of NLP can provide us with the tools to bolster our resilience and refine our coping skills, empowering us to face life's adversities with greater confidence and strength. As we continue to delve deeper into this topic in the upcoming chapters, we'll discover practical ways to leverage NLP to enhance our resilience and improve our coping strategies.

4.1 Cognitive Processes in NLP

NLP is centered around the idea that our thoughts, language, and behaviors are interconnected and influence our experiences of the world. This perspective aligns with the cognitive view in psychology, which asserts that our mental processes (perception, memory, and interpretation) greatly affect our emotions and actions.

Through various techniques, NLP aims to modify these cognitive processes to affect desirable changes. For instance, a technique known as 'reframing' changes the way a person perceives a situation, which can alter their emotional response and subsequent behavior. Another method, 'anchoring', involves associating positive emotional states with specific sensory triggers to induce those states at will.

4.2 Empirical Studies Validating NLP Techniques

Scientific validation of NLP is an ongoing process and can be challenging due to the diversity of techniques and principles it encompasses. While it's true that not all aspects of NLP have been widely studied or empirically supported, there are studies that demonstrate the efficacy of certain NLP techniques.

For example, studies have shown the effectiveness of 'modeling'—a fundamental NLP process in acquiring new skills and behaviors. A study by Charvet (1992) demonstrated that skilled behaviors could be taught more effectively using NLP modeling techniques compared to traditional training methods.

Research on 'reframing', a technique used to change perceptions and responses to a situation, has also found it to be beneficial in cognitive behavioral therapy, often used to treat anxiety and depressive disorders.

It's important to note that while these studies support some of the techniques within NLP, more extensive research is needed to provide a comprehensive evaluation of the overall NLP framework.

4.3 The Impact of NLP on Neuroplasticity

Neuroplasticity refers to the brain's ability to change and adapt as a result of experience. It's the mechanism by which all learning and memory occur. The term 'plasticity' emphasizes that neural connections within the brain can be reorganized through growth and reorganization—something that NLP techniques aim to achieve.

The practice of NLP techniques, such as visualization, anchoring, and reframing, can foster new neural pathways and strengthen existing ones. This is especially relevant when learning new behaviors or changing unhelpful patterns. For instance, consistently applying the 'swish' technique (an NLP method of replacing an unwanted behavior or response with a desired one) can facilitate the development of new neural connections associated with the desired behavior.

It's important to note that the impact of NLP on neuroplasticity is a growing field of study. With advancements in brain imaging technology, we can anticipate more in-depth understanding of this area in the future.

In summary, NLP techniques can influence our cognitive processes and contribute to the ongoing development and adaptability of our brains. While more research is needed to fully elucidate the efficacy and mechanisms of NLP, existing studies and understanding of the brain's plasticity provide a foundation for its potential benefits in enhancing resilience and coping skills.

5.1 The Power of Belief Systems in Resilience

One of the core principles of NLP is that our belief systems play a crucial role in shaping our experiences and behaviors. Beliefs can either advance us or impede us. In the context of resilience, fostering empowering beliefs can significantly contribute to our ability to cope with adversity.

For example, cultivating a belief in one's ability to handle challenges can enhance resilience. This is known as 'self-efficacy' in psychological terms. An NLP technique to nurture this belief is through 'affirmations' and 'self-talk'. By regularly affirming to oneself—either internally or out loud—that they are capable, strong, and adaptable, the individual can gradually shape their belief system in a way that boosts their resilience.

Here's a practical example: Sarah, a young entrepreneur, might be grappling with business challenges. She can employ affirmations like, "I am a problem solver", "I am resilient", and "I can navigate through difficulties". Regular use of such affirmations can fortify her belief in her capability to handle adversity, thereby enhancing her resilience.

5.2 Anchoring: Creating Mental Resilience Touchpoints

'Anchoring' is a technique used in NLP to trigger a specific state of mind or emotion through a sensory cue or 'anchor'. This technique can be a powerful tool for building resilience by anchoring states of calmness, confidence, or strength, which can then be accessed in challenging situations.

For example, John, a public speaker, may feel nervous before speaking engagements. To counteract this, he could use the anchoring technique. He could recall a time when he felt extremely confident and at ease, fully immersing himself in the memory until he re-experiences the positive emotions. At the peak of this positive state, he could create an anchor, such as pressing his thumb and forefinger together. With repetition, this action becomes an anchor for the confident state. So, before a public speaking engagement, John can press his thumb and forefinger together, triggering the anchored confidence, and thereby enhancing his resilience in face of the challenge.

5.3 Future Pacing: Visualization for Resilience

Future pacing is an NLP technique that involves visualizing future situations to prepare oneself mentally and emotionally. It allows us to 'rehearse' for future events in our minds, which can enhance resilience by mentally equipping us to deal with the situation.

For instance, consider Lisa who is apprehensive about an upcoming job interview. To build resilience, Lisa can use future pacing. She can visualize herself going through the interview successfully: answering questions confidently, handling unexpected situations calmly, and leaving the interview feeling accomplished. By rehearsing this in her mind, Lisa can create a positive mental blueprint. When the time for the actual interview arrives, she's likely to feel more resilient, having already 'experienced' a successful outcome in her visualization.

These NLP techniques offer practical ways to enhance resilience. By working on our belief systems, using anchors, and employing visualization, we can equip ourselves better to handle life's adversities, turning challenges into opportunities for growth.

Chapter 6: NLP Techniques for Enhancing Coping Skills

6.1 Reframing: Shifting Perspective for Better Coping

'Reframing' is an NLP technique that involves changing the way we perceive a situation, thus altering our emotional responses and behavior. It can be an effective tool for enhancing coping skills, especially when dealing with adversities or stressors.

For example, Robert, an executive, often feels overwhelmed by his workload. Rather than viewing this as a problem, he could reframe it as an opportunity to develop his time management and delegation skills. This shift in perspective can make the situation seem less threatening and more manageable, improving Robert's ability to cope.

6.2 Metaphor and Storytelling: Creating Positive Narratives

NLP recognizes the power of metaphors and stories in shaping our understanding of the world. By changing our narrative, we can influence our emotions and behaviors, enhancing our coping skills.

Consider Emily, who feels stuck in her current job and views it as a dead-end. She can use metaphor and storytelling to change this narrative. Instead of seeing her job as a 'dead-end', she could perceive it as a 'launchpad' for gaining skills and experiences that will propel her to her next opportunity. This shift in narrative can change her emotional response to her job, improving her ability to cope with the current situation while also fostering hope for the future.

6.3 The Swish Pattern: Redirecting Negative Thoughts

The 'Swish' pattern is an NLP technique designed to replace an unwanted behavior or response with a more desirable one. It can be particularly helpful in enhancing coping skills, especially when it comes to managing negative thoughts or unhelpful reactions to stress.

For instance, every time Alex feels stressed, he tends to resort to binge eating, which negatively impacts his health. Using the Swish technique, he can replace this negative response with a healthier coping mechanism. Each time he feels the urge to binge eat, he visualizes 'swishing' that image away and replacing it with an image of himself engaging in a healthier activity, such as going for a run or meditating. Over time, this technique can help Alex redirect his response to stress, enhancing his coping skills.

By using these NLP techniques—reframing, metaphor and storytelling, and the Swish pattern—we can develop more effective coping skills. Changing our perspective, crafting positive narratives, and redirecting unhelpful behaviors equip us to handle stressors and challenges more effectively, making us not only better at coping, but also more resilient.

All Case Studies Are Hypothetical

7.1 NLP in Therapy: Dealing with Trauma and Stress

NLP techniques have been incorporated into therapeutic practices to help individuals cope with trauma and stress. For instance, the Visual/Kinesthetic Dissociation technique, often referred to as the 'rewind' technique, has been used to treat post-traumatic stress disorder (PTSD). This technique involves mentally 'rewinding' the traumatic event in a safe, dissociated state, which can help reduce the intensity of emotional responses associated with the memory.

In one hypothetical case study, a veteran suffering from PTSD underwent NLP therapy utilizing the rewind technique. Over the course of several sessions, he reported a substantial decrease in the severity of his flashbacks and night terrors. The therapy enabled him to reframe his traumatic experiences, improving his coping abilities and resilience.

7.2 NLP in Business: Enhancing Stress Management and Resilience

In the corporate world, NLP has been used to enhance stress management and resilience among employees. Workshops and training programs employing NLP techniques have helped individuals better cope with workplace stressors.

For instance, a large corporation facing significant restructuring employed NLP coaches to help its employees handle the changes. The coaches taught techniques like reframing, anchoring, and future pacing, to help employees view the changes as opportunities rather than threats. Post-training surveys indicated an improvement in employees' resilience, reduced stress levels, and more positive attitudes towards the changes.

7.3 Personal Stories of Transformation through NLP

NLP has been instrumental in many personal transformation stories. These range from overcoming fears and phobias to developing better communication skills, enhancing self-esteem, and improving overall mental well-being.

One such story involves Maria, a woman suffering from social anxiety. Through a series of NLP sessions, she learned various techniques, including the Swish pattern to replace her anxiety with confidence, and anchoring to trigger a calm state during social interactions. Over time, Maria reported a significant improvement in her social interactions, her anxiety lessened, and her confidence grew. This transformation exemplifies the potential of NLP to enhance coping skills and resilience in everyday life.

These real-life applications and case studies highlight the versatility and effectiveness of NLP in various contexts, from therapy and business to personal development. Whether used to address severe conditions like PTSD, manage workplace stress, or enhance personal growth, NLP holds the potential to significantly improve coping skills and bolster resilience.

8.1 Limitations of NLP

While NLP has shown promise in enhancing resilience and coping skills, it does have its limitations. Firstly, NLP operates on subjective experience and individual perception, which can vary greatly between individuals. This makes it challenging to establish standardized applications of NLP techniques that will be equally effective for everyone.

Secondly, while there are numerous anecdotal accounts and case studies supporting the effectiveness of NLP, there is a lack of extensive empirical research conducted within strict scientific frameworks. This lack of large-scale, controlled, and peer-reviewed studies on NLP has led some to question its validity and effectiveness.

8.2 Addressing the Criticisms and Misconceptions

Critics of NLP argue that it lacks a solid theoretical basis and that its effectiveness is often overstated by practitioners. To address these criticisms, it's essential to view NLP as a toolkit rather than a standalone therapy or a scientific theory. It comprises a collection of techniques that work well in certain contexts and with certain individuals.

Misconceptions often arise from a lack of understanding about what NLP entails. Some see it as a quick fix or a cure-all solution, but in reality, NLP requires active engagement and practice from the individual. Also, the success of NLP is highly dependent on the skill and experience of the practitioner or coach, and their ability to adapt techniques to suit individual needs.

8.3 Guidelines for Ethical and Effective Use of NLP

Given these challenges and critiques, it's vital to follow certain guidelines for the ethical and effective use of NLP.

Transparency: Practitioners should be open about the capabilities and limitations of NLP and avoid overselling it as a miracle solution.

Personalization: NLP techniques should be adapted to the individual's needs, preferences, and context. There's no one-size-fits-all approach.

Professional training: Practitioners should seek robust, professional training to ensure they have a thorough understanding of NLP principles and techniques, and can apply them effectively.

Ongoing research: There's a need for more empirical studies to further validate the effectiveness of NLP and to refine its techniques based on scientific findings.

Understanding the limitations and criticisms of NLP, and adopting a responsible, ethical approach can ensure its effective use in enhancing resilience and coping skills.

9.1 NLP for Self-Improvement: A Daily Guide

NLP can be integrated into daily life as a self-improvement tool. Here's a simple daily guide:

Morning affirmations: Start your day by setting your intention with positive affirmations. If resilience is your goal, affirmations like "I am strong", "I am capable", or "I can handle any challenges today brings" can be effective.

Anchoring: During the day, identify positive states or experiences and create anchors for them. For instance, when you're feeling particularly confident or calm, create a sensory cue (like touching your wrist) that you can use later to recall this state.

Reframing: When faced with challenges, practice reframing. For example, if you're stuck in traffic and starting to feel stressed, reframe this as an opportunity to listen to an audiobook or practice mindfulness.

9.2 Tailoring NLP Techniques to Individual Needs

NLP techniques can and should be personalized to match individual needs and contexts. For instance, someone struggling with social anxiety might find visualization and the Swish technique particularly helpful for managing anxiety triggers. On the other hand, someone aiming to enhance their communication skills may benefit from techniques like mirroring and pacing.

9.3 Tips for Finding and Working with an NLP Practitioner

While self-guided NLP can be beneficial, working with a skilled practitioner can offer personalized guidance and support. Here are a few tips for finding and working with an NLP practitioner:

Credentials and Experience: Look for practitioners with robust NLP training from recognized institutions. Check their experience and areas of expertise to ensure they align with your needs.

Compatibility: Ensure you're comfortable with the practitioner. An initial consultation can help determine if you're a good fit.

Goals and Expectations: Be clear about your goals and expectations for NLP. Discuss these with your practitioner to ensure they can help you achieve them.

Practice and Patience: Remember that NLP is not a quick fix. It requires practice and patience. Be open to trying different techniques and be consistent in your practice.

Integrating NLP into everyday life can be a powerful way to enhance resilience and coping skills. Whether you're exploring NLP for self-improvement or working with a practitioner, remember to tailor the techniques to your needs and to be patient with the process.

10.1 The Emerging Trends in NLP

NLP continues to evolve with emerging trends that seek to broaden its applications and improve its effectiveness. For example, there's an increasing interest in integrating NLP with technology. With the rise of AI and machine learning, developers are exploring ways to incorporate NLP techniques into chatbots and digital therapy platforms, making these tools more personalized and effective.

Another trend is the increasing focus on diversity and cultural sensitivity within NLP. There's a growing recognition of the need to adapt NLP techniques to different cultural contexts and individual backgrounds, acknowledging that one's cultural and personal experiences significantly influence their perception and interpretation of the world.

10.2 Intersection of NLP with Other Therapeutic and Resilience-Enhancing Techniques

NLP is increasingly being integrated with other therapeutic and resilience-enhancing techniques. For instance, combining NLP with mindfulness practices can enhance the power of reframing and visualization techniques. Similarly, integrating NLP with Cognitive Behavioral Therapy (CBT) can provide a more comprehensive approach to managing negative thought patterns.

10.3 The Ongoing and Potential Research on NLP

There's a pressing need for more rigorous research on NLP to validate its techniques and understand how and why they work. As more practitioners and researchers show interest in NLP, we can expect to see an increase in empirical studies.

For example, research could be conducted to investigate the neural mechanisms involved in NLP techniques like anchoring and reframing. Understanding these mechanisms could provide a more solid scientific basis for NLP.

Further, randomized controlled trials could be conducted to measure the efficacy of NLP in enhancing resilience and coping skills, compared to or in combination with other therapeutic approaches. This could help establish best practices for integrating NLP with other therapies.

The future of NLP looks promising, with potential for growth and development in various directions. By continuously evolving and intersecting with other therapeutic techniques, and by conducting rigorous research, NLP holds potential to become an even more powerful tool for enhancing resilience and coping skills.

11.1 Recap of Key Points

Throughout this book, we've embarked on a journey to understand the role of Neuro-Linguistic Programming (NLP) in enhancing resilience and coping skills. We've delved into the history and principles of NLP, dissected the concepts of resilience and coping skills, and highlighted the scientific basis of NLP.

We've explored practical NLP techniques like belief systems, anchoring, future pacing, reframing, and the swish pattern, and shown how they can enhance resilience and coping skills. We also discussed the application of NLP in various real-life contexts, its challenges, and critiques, and offered practical steps to integrate NLP into everyday life.

11.2 The Role of NLP in Enhancing Resilience and Coping Skills

From this exploration, it's clear that NLP plays a significant role in enhancing resilience and coping skills. By offering a set of practical techniques, NLP allows individuals to manage their thoughts, emotions, and behaviors more effectively, helping them handle life's challenges with greater resilience and adaptability.

NLP isn't a quick fix or a magic solution; instead, it's a powerful tool that individuals can use to actively shape their mental processes and behaviors, ultimately leading to enhanced resilience and better coping skills.

11.3 Encouragement for the Journey Ahead

As you continue your journey of self-improvement, remember that change takes time and practice. It's essential to be patient with yourself and maintain a sense of curiosity and openness as you explore and apply NLP techniques.

Whether you're using NLP to enhance your own resilience and coping skills or helping others to do so, remember the power of positive belief systems. Believing in your ability to grow, adapt, and overcome challenges is, in many ways, the first and most crucial step.

Finally, don't forget to celebrate your progress, however small it may seem. Every step you take towards enhancing your resilience and coping skills is a step towards a more balanced, resilient, and fulfilling life.

Rex Morton is a renowned author and researcher in the United Kingdom with a passionate interest in the human mind, specifically in Cognitive Behavioural Therapy (CBT) and Neuro-Linguistic Programming (NLP).

Morton has spent a considerable portion of his professional life diving deep into the theories and principles that form the backbone of these two compelling fields. His fascination with NLP led him to complete an extensive certification program, solidifying his understanding of this innovative approach to understanding human behaviour.

Although Morton does not have clinical experience, his intense curiosity and dedication to studying these subjects have made him a respected figure in the field. He has thoroughly researched the integration of NLP techniques into CBT, offering fresh perspectives and insights into how these two methodologies can complement each other to enhance understanding of human cognition and behaviour.

As an author, Morton has successfully communicated his knowledge and passion to a broader audience, making complex psychological theories accessible to professionals and interested laypersons. His writing is characterized by a clear, engaging style and a focus on the practical application of theories, making them relevant to everyday life.

In his personal life, Morton is an ardent lover of the natural world, often spending his free time exploring the British countryside. His passion for landscape photography allows him to capture and share the beauty of these excursions. Despite his accomplishments, Morton is known for his humility and eagerness to continue learning. His work continues to inspire those interested in the intricate workings of the human mind and the exciting possibilities presented by the integration of NLP and CBT.

If you've found the content of this book enlightening and wish to continue your journey of understanding the human mind, I warmly invite you to visit my website at www.rexmorton.com. The website serves as a hub of knowledge where I share my latest findings, thoughts, and insights on the integration of NLP and CBT.

I also encourage you to subscribe to the newsletter available on the website. By subscribing, you'll receive regular updates on a range of topics, from detailed discussions on specific NLP techniques and their application in CBT, to the latest research in the field.

The newsletter is also the first place I'll share news of upcoming releases. Whether it's the announcement of a new book, the launch of an online course, newsletter subscribers will be the first to know. This is a great opportunity to continue learning directly from me, deepening your understanding of NLP and CBT, and enhancing your skills in applying these techniques in your own life or professional practice.

I'm looking forward to sharing this journey with you.